WHEN
Nature
HEALS

Sunflower (*Helianthus annuus*) ▶

Cover: backlit mule deer at sunrise.

Frontispiece: silhouetted against sunrise light, a mule deer shows the large, broad antler growth commonly found among arsenal bucks. Absence of hunting finds adult male deer with racks that indicate more age than in game populations.

WHEN Nature HEALS

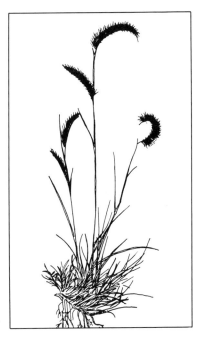

Blue Grama (*Bouteloua gracilis*) ▶

The Greening Of
ROCKY MOUNTAIN ARSENAL

Photographs by
WENDY SHATTIL
AND
BOB ROZINSKI

Essay by
CHRIS MADSON

Drawings by
Paula Nicholas

ROBERTS RINEHART, INC.
PUBLISHERS
in cooperation with the
NATIONAL FISH AND
WILDLIFE FOUNDATION

CONTENTS

Sand Lily

(*Leucocrinum montanum*) ▶

◀ Great blue heron. A great blue heron stands motionless in water until the time is right to strike. More often than not it will come away with its prey, in this case a carp caught in a marshy pond.

Note: the views of the author are his own, and do not represent those of the book's sponsor, photographers or publishers.

Text © 1990 by Chris Madson
Photographs © 1990 by Wendy Shattil and Robert Rozinski
Published by Roberts Rinehart, Inc. Publishers
Post Office Box 3161 Boulder, Colorado 80303

International Standard Book Number 0-911797-71-8
Library of Congress Catalog Card Number 89-64061
Printed in the United States of America
Designed by Ann W. Douden

Publication of this book was made possible through the generous assistance of the Shell Oil Company, the National Fish and Wildlife Foundation, and Hunter Environmental Services, Inc.

PREFACE AND ACKNOWLEDGMENTS

Western Yarrow

(*Achillea lanulosa*) ▶

◀ *Burrowing owl perched on yucca.*

An adult burrowing owl views the

arsenal from its high perch.

The strategy for producing toxic materials at Rocky Mountain Arsenal was unique for its time, in that production was isolated in the center of the post, allowing a vast, undeveloped area to serve as a buffer zone. Once production ended at the arsenal the buffer areas attracted and protected a burgeoning wildlife population. The purpose of this book is to document and inform readers about the population of wild things living literally within the shadow of Denver.

Rocky Mountain Arsenal has emerged as a significant habitat island for wildlife; with proper care not to unbalance the ecosystem, it can develop as a refuge for a human population seeking escape from the artificial world we've created. We envision the arsenal as a place to renew our relationship with nature and to observe and learn from a harmonious working ecosystem.

Large parcels of land such as the arsenal, nearby Stapleton Airport, Buckley Field, and Lowry Air Force Base have become increasingly vital to many wildlife species. For such species as mammals, they are simply isolated areas of existence. For others, they are part of an ecological chain, as raptors, for example, fly from one parcel of land to another in search of food.

We have photographed wildlife throughout the American West from Wyoming to the Texas gulf coast, as well as in Alaska and Africa. With the possible exception of East Africa, we

know of no area of comparable size possessed of the diversity and density of wildlife that exists at Rocky Mountain Arsenal. The sheer numbers of animals inhabiting this land provided us with the opportunity to observe and photograph in a single year behavior that otherwise would have required much more field time.

Despite years of study there was previously little photo documentation of the arsenal animals. The existence and extent of the wildlife certainly was unknown to the general public. Not until the United States Fish & Wildlife Service became a presence on the site did a method emerge to acquaint people with the phenomenon. Public tours, a visitor center, and an eagle observation point were instituted. At the request of the Army and Fish & Wildlife we were given the task of documenting images of the remarkable wildlife that has been quietly living in our urban community. It is thanks to the United States Army, not typi-

cally thought of as addressing concerns of wildlife, that programs have been put into action that anticipate the ongoing needs of key species.

The fact that a thriving wildlife population exists despite contamination and clean-up activities portends tremendous potential for the area. It is impossible to observe wildlife at the arsenal and not come away with a renewed hope that our damage to the land is reversible and salvageable. The animals have found the food, shelter, and range they require. They have chosen this territory as home.

The future of Rocky Mountain Arsenal is uncertain. We hope when you have finished this book you will tour the site and add your voice to the eagle's cry, the deer's grunts, the prairie dog's alarm call, the owl's hoot, and the coyote's howl to assure that this extraordinary spot remains the sanctuary it has become.

*Wendy Shattil
Robert Rozinski*

We wish to acknowledge with thanks the assistance of the following organizations and individuals, without whose support publication of this book would not have been possible: Colonel Wallace Quintrell and Colonel Daniel Voss of the United States Army; Pete Gober and Mike Lockhart and the other supporting members of the United States Fish & Wildlife Service; Chip Collins and Whitney Tilt of the National Fish and Wildlife Foundation; Denver Audubon Society; Colorado Wildlife Federation; Hunter Environmental Services, Inc.; the National Wildlife Federation; Ann Douden; Paula Nicholas; and Betsy Webb.

Thanks also to the countless people who have responded with vision to the presence of wildlife at Rocky Mountain Arsenal, as well as to members of the media who have provided exemplary coverage of this developing story.

*Chris Madson
Robert Rozinski
Wendy Shattil*

 Bald eagle against skyline. A stunning aspect of the arsenal and its wildlife is the proximity to downtown Denver. Not many Denverites are aware that they have bald eagles as neighbors.

WHEN
Nature
HEALS

9

◀ *Deer and flagpole. Mule deer*

graze the grass and browse shrubs

while travelling past arsenal

headquarters.

FOREWORD

Sand Verbena

(*Abronia fragrans*) ▶

During my ten-year tenure in the State of Colorado, from 1973-1982, I shared the same perception as most of Colorado's citizenry about the Rocky Mountain Arsenal: that the arsenal was a toxic wasteland contaminated by its use as a chemical weapons manufacturing facility during World War II and later as a pesticide plant.

Though I had spent four years as Director of the Colorado field office of The Nature Conservancy, which included serving on Governor Lamm's Front Range project, I was as surprised as anyone when I began to see articles in the local and national press about the exceptional wildlife values purported to exist at the arsenal. Was this a public relations smokescreen designed to mask the serious problems that existed, or was it in fact true that the arsenal supported herds of trophy-sized mule and white-tailed deer? Was it really one of the most significant bald eagle wintering sites on the Front Range?

I finally got to see the arsenal firsthand at the invitation of the US Fish and Wildlife Service in September of 1989. We drove through the gates on a grey, drizzly day and passed, at a distance, the eerie abandoned gas and chemical facility. I overcame my initial nervousness about whether I should be clothed in a protective suit as we moved out over the prairie lands. We spent the day touring the site, and while it was too early for the eagles, I saw an extremely impressive array of wildlife, particularly when viewed against the backdrop of the Denver skyline. A wealth of raptors, songbirds, deer and other species were present. These images have been captured between the covers of this book.

I came away from this visit convinced that the arsenal is indeed a wildlife treasure worthy of conserving and restoring. To be sure, it has serious problems that will take years to resolve. Yet the arsenal is a unique and invaluable resource for the citizens of the Denver metropolitan area and the rest of Colorado. The arsenal's challenges embody society's most pressing problems and needs—to clean up our toxic waste and manage development pressures brought on by our ever-burgeoning population while protecting our sensitive natural resources. The arsenal can serve as a model—a model for the State of Colorado and the rest of our nation. It is a resource that we can not lose.

I hope readers of this book will capture the sense of excitement and challenge that the arsenal offers, and help to conserve the unique wildlife and open space attributes of this twenty-seven-square-mile anomaly while ensuring the health and safety risks are put behind us.

Charles H. Collins,
Executive Director, National
Fish and Wildlife Foundation

WHEN NATURE HEALS

An Essay by Chris Madson

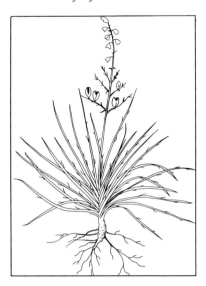

Yucca, Soapweed, Spanish

Bayonet (*Yucca glauca*) ▶

◀ *Turkey vultures roosting in dead*

tree. With Denver's downtown

skyline just visible through the

trees, a vulture stretches its

wings—an early morning ritual.

A driver on the elevated slab of Interstate 70 sees a reasonably accurate cross-section of the city—the upscale glass and evergreens of foothills office complexes, the regimented neatness of middle-class suburbs, the steam clouds and gray patina of old factories, the broken ridgelines and leaking roofs of abandoned houses under the highway, fast food, fast gas, fast traffic, great wealth, poverty, all under a blue sky that fades away to a faint brown at the horizon. The Rocky Mountain Front is an unusual backdrop, but Denver itself is not so different from a hundred other metropoli scattered across the continent, hurrying toward an ideal no one has really stopped to define. It's an unlikely place to contemplate a basic truth: that time is a shaper of land as well

as men. Not long ago, even as the city would count the years, this was a different place.

Stephen Long's men rested here in the summer of 1820, sunburned and weatherbeaten from a month's ride across the high grasslands, worn out from too much wind and sky. They gave thanks for the humble amenities they found here.

"Our camp is beautifully situated on the bank of the river," their diarist wrote, "which here is about 100 yards wide— our tents are pitched in a grove of cottonwood trees that shade us from the scorching rays of the sun."

A couple of decades later, a young Bostonian, Francis Parkman, rode the same way.

"About noon on that day we reached Cherry Creek. Here was a great abundance of wild-cherries, plums, gooseberries, and currants."

And later, in the winter of 1868, when the currants and cottonwoods along Cherry Creek had already given way to offices and trollies, the essence of the country still lingered. Major J. B. Pond, a passenger on the new rail line between Denver and Cheyenne, recalled this scene: "All the Antelope had left the open plains, and were now sheltering among the foothills. For 10 or 12 miles . . . and all the way west of the train . . . was one long band of Antelope, 20 to 40 rods wide, practically continuous, and huddled together for warmth.

Their numbers changed the colour of the country."

The transformation occurred almost overnight. By the turn of the century, the wilderness of the high plains had been brought to heel and, in two generations more, forgotten. Most modern Denverites regard the 500 miles of emptiness to the east of the city limits as a necessary evil, the price a traveler has to pay to get from Kansas City to the Front Range.

The prairie, however, has a different view. Its sod broken, its grass pounded to dust under too many tame hooves, its ridges stitched over with barbed wire and telephone lines, the prairie still refuses to

die. Given an unplowed corner of ground and some time, it reasserts a little of the old wildness. The proof of this persistence is sometimes found in unusual places . . . places like Rocky Mountain Arsenal.

Until 1942, the arsenal was a fairly typical piece of hard-scratch prairie ranch country, grazed by a variety of livestock, plowed for dryland wheat. The history of the caretakers, their aspirations and mistakes, is broadly recorded here, as it is recorded across most of the high plains, in the vegetation. A third of the area inside the arsenal fences has been claimed by cheatgrass, an Asian native that thrives in the wake of persistent overgrazing. The great grandsons of the

Sand Dropseed

(*Sporobolus cryptandrus*) ▶

Needle-and-Thread

(*Stipa comata*) ▶

◀ *Bobwhite on detour sign. Recent activities such as dog trials and a gun club allowed non-traditional species a chance to adapt to this prairie habitat. Although northern bobwhite are native to Colorado, it is likely that the population at the arsenal owes its origin to deliberate introductions.*

men who first left ten cows on this pasture where there should have been one probably wouldn't recognize the difference between these stands of cheat and the buffalo grass and blue grama they replaced. Pressed to account for the failure of the family ranch, they would probably explain it as a run of bad luck.

A number of other aggressive Old World natives have followed the cheat onto the arsenal—bindweed, prickly lettuce, summer-cypress, Canada thistle—all indicators of major disturbances in the past. There are even some native plants here—rabbitbrush and scarlet globemallow, among others—that have profited by the abuse of the ground. But, plow and cow notwithstanding, the prairie here persisted. Mixed in with the invaders and occasionally continuing as fairly pristine stands in their own right are many of the original members of the prairie community. Three-awn, sand dropseed, and needle-and-thread show signs of invading the invader as the cheatgrass loses the advantage it once gained from overgrazing. And about a fifth of the arsenal can still be classified as "native grassland" with extensive stands of blue grama and western wheatgrass, along with other native species.

Down along First Creek, the offspring of Stephen Long's plains cottonwoods are sixty feet tall or more, still furnishing the same welcome shade their ancestors provided in 1820. On damper sites, peach-leaf willow, another Great Plains native, edges the creek.

All in all a very ordinary tract of the high plains, these twenty-seven square miles were set apart as a result of a Depression-era city promotion and a world war.

As early as 1921, the federal government had a substantial presence in Denver, buying an estimated $3.5 million worth of supplies in that year alone. By the early Thirties, influential members of the Chamber of Commerce had recognized the importance of the federal dollar in Denver and set out to get as much Congressional appropriation as they could lay their hands on. They called it the "Little Capitol" or "Second Capitol" campaign in recognition of their vision of

Denver as a western version of Washington, D.C.

Denver leaders beat a path to Washington through the late Thirties, and, as the decade drew to a close, the effort began to pay off. A new Army Air Corps technical school was loacted in Denver followed late in 1940 by a small arms plant which many Washington observers had wanted on the east coast closer to the European war. Then, in 1942, the Rocky Mountain Arsenal came to town.

▲

Aerial view of the South Plants (1989). With downtown Denver and the Front Range in the dis- *tance, this view graphically illus-trates the arsenal's proximity to the urban area.*

The original mission of the facility was to manufacture mustard gas and other chemical weapons for the war effort. At the peak of its wartime operations, the arsenal employed 14,000 people. The manufacturing plants and rail depots were located in the middle of 19,000 acres of fallow farm and ranch land, partly for security, partly for the safety of nearby residents. Unneeded by-products of the chemical processes at the plants were shunted into a natural basin and forgotten.

After the war, the Army used the arsenal to develop and manufacture new chemical and biological weapons as well as to un-manufacture weapons it had already built. Stockpiles of mustard gas, chlorine gas, phosgene, arsenic chloride, cyanogen chloride, incendiary bombs, and 107-millimeter mortar shells were routinely destroyed there.

Beginning in 1947, private manufacturers leased facilities on the arsenal for the production of a variety of chemicals, especially pesticides. The manifest of products includes most of the notorious insecticides of the late Sixties and Seventies—DDT, chlordane, aldrin, dieldrin, endrin, parathion. Other potentially dangerous chemicals like chlorine, caustic, anti-icers, curing agents, and oil additives weren't produced at the ar-

▲

Meadowlark on sign. This was the traditional public view of the arsenal; it was not intended to be an inviting place for people or wildlife. However, education has enlightened humans to the merit of undeveloped land and its significance to wildlife populations.

senal but were used in the manufacturing process. The toxic by-products of the Army and private manufacturers were deposited in the original waste basin until it was full, then in a series of additional ponds.

As dangerous as operations at the core of the arsenal were, they had little effect on wildlife in the surrounding buffer zones. These outlying areas offered relatively undisturbed quarters with a variety of native and introduced food and cover types. The growth of wild populations was immediate.

As early as 1955, maintenance people on the arsenal reported using Compound 1080 to control a burgeoning population of black-tailed prairie dogs. The fragmentary records of "pest" control efforts on the arsenal don't describe the effect of that first poisoning or the persistence the maintenance crew showed in their pursuit, but the dogs were still thriving on the arsenal in 1976 when plague was discovered in the fleas of at least one prairie dog town on the area. Managers decided that, in the interest of the health of nearby homeowners, a thousand acres of prairie dog town should be poisoned. The campaign claimed an estimated 6,000 prairie dogs and was followed by less ambitious prairie dog control mea-

▲

Prairie dog colony. The greatest attraction for winter predators at the arsenal is the large population of black-tailed prairie dogs. Numbers were estimated at 40,000 in 1988 but have since declined.

sures through the decade of the 1980s. The effect of three decades of these prairie dog wars has been equivocal—a survey in 1987 estimated that prairie dog colonies covered about 5,000 acres of the arsenal. That's somewhere in the vicinity of 50,000 prairie dogs. An outbreak of plague in 1988 decimated the population, but, if these dogs follow the pattern of the breed in other parts of the West, it's unlikely that the losses will have any long-term effect on their numbers.

Less visible but no less important in the fabric of the prairie community, a number of other small mammals began a comeback on the arsenal. Cottontail rabbits, white- and black-tailed jackrabbits, deer mice, harvest mice, the predatory grasshopper mouse, voles, kangaroo rats, pocket gophers, and ground squirrels have been recorded in surveys over the years. These grazers and gleaners aren't the kind of wildlife that awed nineteenth-century visitors to the high grasslands, but, along with the grass itself, they are the foundation on which more famous prairie natives depend. It was the arrival of these higher-profile tenants that first alerted conservationists to the real value of the arsenal.

▲

Row of prairie dogs. Although they generally have only one litter each year, prairie dogs appear prolific because of large broods and aggressive colonization.

The Hawks

Ferruginous hawk taking flight. During winter, dozens of ferruginous hawks may roost communally overnight in groves of trees. ▶

◀ *Cottontail washing next to truck. It is typical for wildlife in urban settings such as the arsenal to adapt their needs to their surroundings, as evidenced by this rabbit grooming in the shelter of a parked truck.*

"Regalis" the taxonomists have named it, and the ferruginous hawk richly deserves the title. Largest of North America's hawks, the ferruginous rides the prairie's thermals on wings that may span five feet, making a living almost exclusively on rodents and rabbits. One of the twentieth century's leading ornithologists, Arthur Cleveland Bent, was enthusiastic in his praise of the species: "One who knows it in life," he wrote, "cannot help being impressed with its close relationship to the golden eagle. . . . Both species have feathered tarsi, both build huge nests on cliffs or trees, and both lay eggs that are very similar except in size; the food habits, flight, behavior, and voice of the two are much alike."

The ferruginous hawk is a grassland specialist. Breeding pairs will build their nests in cottonwoods where they are available, but the lack of trees doesn't keep them from establishing a nursery. A typical ferruginous nest occupies most of a rock pinnacle or ledge on a prairie rim or badlands outcrop. The nest itself is built of branches and small limbs, usually of sagebrush or yucca since the nearest true timber may be dozens of miles away. There are records of wild ferruginous hawks living for twenty years, and it appears that they return to their nests year after year, adding material each breeding season, finally creating a structure up to fifteen feet deep and six feet across.

Like most prairie natives, the ferruginous hawk dotes on the wide open spaces, especially while raising a family. Research done in Idaho indicates that breeding pairs never learn to tolerate human presence near their nests; in fact, they seem to become more skittish with each disturbance. While the parents don't seem inclined to abandon their nests, they do stay away for hours after a human visit. The young are left exposed to rain and other predators and are probably not fed as often. As a result, disturbed nests seldom produce as many fledglings as undisturbed sites.

Unfortunately, disturbance is an all-too-common event at ferruginous hawk nests. These highly visible structures routinely draw attention from passers-by. Some vandals make a practice of shooting the adults on their nests, killing valuable allies in the ongoing farm struggle with rodents. But, as the researchers have proved, it doesn't take shooting to cancel a nest's contribution to the future of the species. Just the visit can be enough.

The uncertainty of success at the nest is in itself a serious threat to the well-being of ferruginous hawks, but it is by no means the only difficulty the species faces. On the northern edge of its range in southern Alberta, the ferruginous is faced with a steady erosion of its habitat. Control of fire at the northern edge of the

▲

Ferruginous hawk confrontation.

When a hawk captures prey, it is

soon joined by other raptors hop-

ing for a portion of the kill. As a

feeding bird becomes satiated, it

eventually gives way when one of

the hungrier birds approaches.

prairie has allowed aspen forest to move south, eliminating forty percent of the bird's breeding in the province. And investigations in that area have turned up a second habitat change that has had far more widespread effect on the hawk throughout its breeding range—cultivation. The breaking of native prairie sod may eliminate preferred ferruginous hawk prey, or it may simply make hunting more difficult. Whatever the specific cause, Alberta researchers have found that ferruginous hawks avoid regions of the prairie which are more than half plowed. The trend toward cultivation of the High Plains throughout North America has almost certainly deprived the species of critically needed hunting and breeding territory.

Migration is a dangerous exercise for any creature, but it is particularly hazardous for young ferruginous hawks. One pair of biologists estimates that two-thirds of the immature birds banded in southwestern Canada died in their first year. Other researchers have pointed out that ferruginous hawks are exposed to high levels of pesticides on their winter range in Mexico and may suffer from the same kinds of reproductive failures that once decimated bald eagles, ospreys, and peregrine falcons in the U.S.

There is no doubt that ferruginous hawk populations have lost ground in the last century. It's been estimated that there

▲

Ferruginous hawk landing. Large numbers of ferruginous hawks frequent the arsenal. This species greatly benefits wintering bald eagles by catching prairie dogs but abandoning them when confronted by an eagle looking for a meal.

are only 3,000 to 4,000 nesting pairs of ferruginous hawks left in North America. As early as 1937, Bent commented that "the ignorant prejudice against all hawks has reduced this useful species to the verge of extinction . . ." In 1972, it was included on the Audubon Society's Blue List of birds in jeopardy of becoming officially threatened or endangered. It is also listed by the U.S. Fish and Wildlife Service as a "category 2 species," meaning that there is some information which could support listing of the bird as officially "threatened."

During the winter, ferruginous hawks are the most common bird of prey at the Rocky Mountain Arsenal. Counts have turned up populations of more than a hundred of the birds, most of them immature, hunting prairie dog towns on the north and west sides of the arsenal. Although these dog towns are only a shadow of the original article on the High Plains, they are more dependable than surviving dog towns on private holdings. Many counties in the plains states periodically insist that private landholders "control" prairie dogs on their property with poison. If the landholder doesn't uphold his responsibility, the county often carries out control work on its own and charges the owner for the work. With this system in place, a thriving dog town can disappear overnight.

The arsenal attracts ferruginous hawks for another reason as well. Some of the best remaining ferruginous habitat is in central Wyoming and Montana. Hawks raised in these regions run into the central Colorado high country on their way south in the fall. Many of the birds detour east, coming at last to the Front Range which they follow south, headed for the flat country of western Texas, eastern New Mexico, and points south. The arsenal offers a good alternative to longer migration with plenty of protein and a winter climate that is tolerable, at least from a hawk's point of view.

The dense population of hawks offers unusual opportunities for observing behavior. The ferruginous is known for at least one rather unorthodox hunting technique. It was described in 1893 by an ornithologist in western Montana: "The methods of the crafty coyote and the ferruginous rough-leg are identical in 'dog-towns.' Both wait patiently, the hawk also on the ground, for a prairie dog to amble afield from its burrow, and thereupon make a dash, the first terrestrial, the latter aerial, to intercept it. A prairie dog always endeavors to gain its own burrow when danger threatens, and is marvelously quick to reach it, but if cut off from home, the beast becomes so bewildered that it neglects the nearer intermediate holes. When two coyotes, or two hawks hunt together, the fate of the intended victim is sealed, but with one assailant only, it has an even chance." This ground-based style is common among the arsenal's ferruginous hawks; the birds can frequently be seen loitering near a prairie dog hole, waiting to greet any resident foolish enough to stick up his head.

Coyote hunting. Coyotes are the ultimate example of a generalist predator. A generalist is capable of adapting to a variety of conditions and utilizing whatever food source is most available. ▶

Two coyotes. Coyotes often hunt in pairs or small packs when additional numbers increase the chance of success. They are intelligent and very adaptable, thriving on the abundance of prey at the arsenal. ▶

The Eagles

Bald eagle profile. The U.S. Fish & Wildlife Service attached a radio transmitter to this bird in order to monitor its movements while it wintered at the arsenal. ▶

◀ *Golden eagle on chimney. An abandoned barracks provides a convenient perch site for a wintering golden eagle.*

A few creatures on this planet are endowed from their first breath with a special charisma. They draw an audience when nothing else can and leave the crowd breathless when the show is over. They're stars, recognized by the tenderest school kid and the most confirmed indoorsman. The bald eagle is near the top of that elite list.

The imposing figure of the bird may have something to do with its reputation. Three-and-a-half feet tall with a wing span approaching eight feet, a bald eagle passing close overhead gives the impression of a low-flying Cessna. And the incandescent white of the adult's head and tail is beautiful, especially when it is magnified against the flawless blue of a winter sky. Because of this plumage, the adult bald eagle may be the most universally recognized bird on the continent, and as the public relations hacks have taught us in recent presidential elections, name recognition is a critical part of any popularity contest.

But the legend is far more than just physique. The bald eagle is a symbol, not only of the most powerful nation on earth but of the wilderness that has been the source of that power. There is some truth in the conviction held by most Americans that the bald eagle lives only in the most pristine back country. When a pair of bald eagles chooses a nesting site, a key consideration is lack of human disturbance. Some students of bald eagles have stated that the birds will not tolerate an obvious human presence within a mile of a nest. While this is not always true—as evidenced by the successful bald eagle nest at Barr Lake, four miles north of the arsenal—it is an indication of the eagle's preference for seclusion while raising a family.

Wintering bald eagles are a little less sensitive about people.

Eagles congregate below dams on the Mississippi and its tributaries to eat fish killed by the passage through the gates; they follow migrating waterfowl and winter where the flocks winter. City dwellers near these concentration areas are generally amazed to find that there are bald eagles within an hour or two of their front porches. The surprise is partly due to the presence of the bird itself and

partly to the presence of that vestige of wildness the bird represents.

Denver's city dwellers have an unusually convenient opportunity to see the national bird in the flesh. In 1988, up to 100 bald eagles took up winter residence at Rocky Mountain Arsenal. Until last winter, this congregation was off-limits to all but a handful of people who

▲

Bald eagles in tree. In winter bald eagles often roost communally at night and occasionally perch to-gether during the day. Individuals tend to use the same branch re-peatedly, and disputes arise if that site is occupied.

had clearance to enter the arsenal, but thanks to the Army, the Denver Audubon Society, and the U.S. Fish and Wildlife Service, the general public now has a chance to take a look. These organizations have rented a double-decker tour bus for wildlife tours through the winter. During the first winter of the tours in 1988–89, more than 1,500 people signed up to see the eagles. Twice that number came to see the arsenal's wildlife in the winter of 1989–90.

After seeing a treeful of eagles within a mile of Denver-Stapleton airport and Interstate 70, a casual observer could easily assume that the rumor of the bald eagle's demise has been greatly exaggerated. But the decline of the eagle is no rumor. At one time, these birds could be found across the continent. There is solid evidence that bald eagles once nested in at least forty-six of the contiguous states. But pressure on eagle populations began almost as soon as the first settlers arrived. As early as 1668, settlers in Maine shot "an infinite number" of eagles to feed to their hogs. By 1921, ornithologists were predicting extinction for the bird if some-

▲

Golden eagle flying from branch.

The embodiment of strength,

power, and beauty, a golden eagle

is a majestic sight at Rocky Moun-

tain Arsenal.

thing wasn't done to halt indiscriminate killing and ongoing destruction of habitat.

Then, to add to the species' problems, something went wrong with bald eagle reproduction in the late Forties. Numbers of young eagles plummeted, even though adult pairs continued to go through the motions of raising families. More than a decade of research finally revealed the cause—DDT and other persistent pesticides concentrated through the food web, thinning eagle eggshells so much that they broke before hatching.

Beginning in 1940 with the passage of the Bald Eagle Protection Act, state and federal wildlife managers and many private-sector conservationists have taken a series of steps to protect the national bird from these threats to its future. The results have been heartening. In 1962, only 515 pairs of nesting bald eagles were reported in the contiguous forty-eight states. In 1982, that number had increased to 1,482 nesting pairs. While a significant part of that increase is due to better survey work rather than an increase in actual population, there is little doubt that our eagles are making a recovery. Winter counts in the U.S. have turned up as many as 14,000 bald eagles. Biologists guess that three-fourths of these birds are migrants from Canada and Alaska, but that still means that some 3,500 eagles are year-round residents of the coterminous U.S.

In December 1988, the Army established a special bald eagle management area along the First Creek drainage on the east side of the arsenal. The cottonwoods along the creek were one of the key attractions for the eagles, providing plenty of high perches with a good view of the country in every direction, an excellent spot to loaf away the day or spend the night. The birds forage for miles along the South Platte River, and as they have become more familiar with their winter quarters, they have found an unexpected additional food source closer to home. Bald eagles are masters at intimidating smaller raptors and stealing the fruits of their labor. The classic confrontation reported in the literature is between the eagle and a fish-carrying osprey, the osprey bullied by the larger bird until it drops the fish which the eagle often catches before it hits the water. The arsenal doesn't attract many ospreys, but it does have a large contingent of ferruginous hawks, most of which have developed prairie dog killing to a fine art. This unusual set of circumstances has given the Rocky Mountain Arsenal eagles a certain degree of notoriety in wildlife management circles—they may be the only members of their species on the continent that have set aside their taste for fish and fowl to winter on a diet of fresh prairie dog. The fact that the main course is obtained and unwillingly served by a succession of young ferruginous hawks doesn't seem to give the big birds the least twinge of conscience.

▲

Black-tailed prairie dog gathering   their burrows.

grass. In late fall prairie dogs can

be seen collecting grass to line

The Deer

Running whitetail buck. White-tailed deer are less abundant than mule deer at the arsenal; they are also more secretive and prefer denser cover.

Dashing through the riparian habitat near the arsenal's lakes, a mule deer goes to join the rest of a bachelor herd. ▶

◀ *Sparring mule deer does. Through this behavior these deer may be reinforcing their positions within the herd, or they may simply be playing.*

In the fall of 1891, sportsman Ernest Ingersoll reflected on the changes he had seen along the Rocky Mountain Front with some nostalgia. "Only fifteen years ago," he wrote, "deer might easily be shot within sight of Denver, Colorado Springs, or Canon City. . . . This primitive condition of things has been greatly modified."

It's easy to lose sight of the "primitive condition" after all these years, to assume, as many westerners do, that mule deer have always preferred the security of the high country to the exposed vistas of the grasslands below. The fact of the matter is that the plains once supported a thriving deer population. These open-country deer were inclined to spend their entire lives in the broken ravines and streamside timber of the grasslands.

Plains mule deer nearly disappeared in the first decades of the twentieth century. Market hunting in the 1890s set the stage for disaster, but settlement of the High Plains probably had more to do with the collapse of deer populations than any other factor. Farmers and ranchers rushed to claim the last of the American frontier, crowding the grasslands with small operations that were doomed to failure. Overgrazing, overplowing, the desperate struggle to grow corn and wheat where corn and wheat could not grow—the marks of the homesteaders still linger on the land. The end for most operations came with the drought of the Thirties, six years of dust that reasserted the high grassland's brand of reality. Following the Dust Bowl, mule deer populations began to recover across the Great Plains, reaching a broad peak in the late Sixties and early Seventies.

Cover is a critical part of mule deer habitat, especially on the Plains. Muleys aren't terribly picky about their menus—a wide variety of shrubs, grasses, and forbs will support a mule deer herd. But excessive disturbance and a lack of cover will keep deer out of a given piece of real estate. Deer obviously need a measure of security from a variety of predators. In addition, they need shelter from the elements. The slightest difference in temperature or wind chill can make the difference between survival and an untimely death over the course of a prairie winter.

Fallow land on the arsenal offers cover for nearly every occasion as well as ample forage, so it should come as no surprise that biologists have counted more than 300 mule deer on the area. Many of these animals stay year-round, but a surprising number move in and out, following natural corridors like First Creek or

▲

Mule deer bucks in velvet. Bachelor herds of bucks roam large areas of the arsenal for most of the year. At quick glance this tight-knit band could almost be mistaken for a row of shrubs.

traveling overland from the northeast and occasionally from the southwest out of the city. The urban development around the arsenal isn't the kind of habitat they prefer, but it is by no means an impenetrable barrier. Except for encounters with traffic on some of the local thoroughfares, deer move back and forth unnoticed by most local residents.

Native cottonwood-willow thickets on the arsenal provide shade in the worst heat of the summer and shelter from winter wind. Some shade-hungry owner of a long-abandoned farmstead planted locust to help shut out the prairie wind, and the shrub has since claimed ninety acres, mostly on the south side of the arsenal, a particularly dense stand of escape cover for deer, especially the small group of white-tails that share the arsenal with their western cousins. Muleys on the area spend much of their time bedded down in huge fields of thistle and cheatgrass, completely hidden from prying eyes except when they stand up for a look around.

Then there is the equipment shed east of the south plant complex. Built of corrugated sheet steel and about fifty

▲

Does and fawns in frost. Heavy

winter coats insulate deer from the

Colorado cold. Groves of trees and

heavy thickets provide shelter, but

deer must forage in open areas to

find much of their food.

yards long, the shed is open to the air on its south side. It's down in a swale well off the main road, a secluded, if not very handsome, spot. On a summer morning not too long ago, I was making the rounds of the arsenal with photographers Wendy Shattil and Bob Rozinski who begged my indulgence for a stop at the shed. They wanted to set up a remote camera there, they said.

"What for?" I inquired innocently.

"Deer," they said with straight faces. "Lots of them."

Hanging around with biologists, freelance photographers, and other such puckish characters as long as I have, I've slowly developed a healthy skepticism.

"Right," I commented dryly.

We walked in under the tin roof onto a floor of fine dust. It was covered with delicate cloven tracks. I apologized to Wendy and Bob for my lack of trust and reflected again on the adaptability of the average mule deer.

▲

In the intense heat of summer, mule deer have been seen taking shelter in this abandoned utility shed. Occasionally there were dozens of deer relishing the shade, at first glance resembling stabled horses.

Surrounded by agriculture, airport, and industry, the arsenal is a habitat oasis for species such as the mule deer. ▶

◄ *Heron reflection. As ponds evapo-*

rate during summer, the decreas-

ing water concentrates fish and

other food. Great blue herons and

shorebirds (such as this sandpiper)

often share this rich bonanza.

Others

Badgers are much faster than they appear. Their speed combined with a difficult-to-grasp loose skin make them a formidable foe for any enemy, including the rattlesnake. ▶

The roster of wildlife on the Rocky Mountain Arsenal is far more extensive than this, of course. Prairie dogs on the area have attracted their usual coterie of camp followers. Badgers and coyotes join the ferruginous hawks in a largely ineffective effort to keep the dog colonies thinned out. In summer, one of the Great Plains' most curious birds of prey, the burrowing owl, sets up nurseries in abandoned tunnels in the dog towns. This little hunter is too small to take prairie dogs and feeds its young on meadow voles, deer mice, and grasshoppers. A prairie-dwelling friend of mine fondly refers to burrowing owls as "little soldiers," and there is some resemblance— standing in the close-cropped grass of a dog town, the owls

have the chesty, wedge-shaped profile of a drill sergeant in dress blouse. In fact, this top-heavy look is the best way to tell the difference between the owls and nearby upright prairie dogs, who sit on the bulk of their weight.

In the summer of 1988, a swift fox raised a den of pups in one of the toxic storage yards, and swifts are regularly reported on the arsenal. The swift is the smallest and, to my eye, easily the most graceful of the fox clan. A thirteen-lined ground squirrel is big game for this tiny canine. Hardly bigger than a house cat, it routinely preys on mice and insects and avoids becoming prey itself with its talent as a sprinter. In the long campaign against coyotes, the swift fox has been an unin-

tended casualty. Unlike the coyote, the swift never seemed to figure out the difference between honest carrion and strychnine- and 1080-laced baits. As a result, swifts became a rare sight on the central plains through the 1960s and 1970s, so much so that there was talk of adding them to the federal endangered species list. Happily, the ban on 1080 has given the species a breathing spell and it seems to have bounced back.

The swift is joined on the arsenal by its larger brethren, the highly successful red fox and the gray fox, a largely nocturnal, tree-loving hunter. All three of the fox species live in uneasy association with the area's coyotes which will take the smaller canids as prey

WHEN
Nature
HEALS

39

when the opportunity presents itself.

Most of the common high plains birds are also on the arsenal: horned larks, meadowlarks, lark buntings, lark sparrows, vesper sparrows—all the bright voices that embroider the heat of a prairie summer. The thickets of locust and willow attract a variety of other birds as well—woodpeckers, sparrows, warblers, vireos, magpies, orioles, and flycatchers either breed here or pass through on migration.

Then there are the birds that are drawn to water, a diverse, highly visible crowd given to long trips and short stays. Chief among them are the ducks and geese. Nineteen species have been reported on the arsenal, from Canada geese to green-winged teal. Few people think of the web-footed clan as prairie birds, but the majority of them nest and raise their broods on the mixed grass prairies of the northcentral U.S. and southern Canada.

▲

Badger at edge of hole. Possessing great strength and determination, the badger is an efficient predator of small mammals and ground-nesting birds. At the arsenal its primary prey are prairie dogs. A balanced predator-prey relationship reflects a healthy ecosystem.

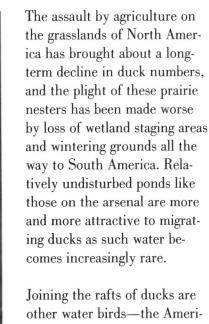

The assault by agriculture on the grasslands of North America has brought about a long-term decline in duck numbers, and the plight of these prairie nesters has been made worse by loss of wetland staging areas and wintering grounds all the way to South America. Relatively undisturbed ponds like those on the arsenal are more and more attractive to migrating ducks as such water becomes increasingly rare.

Joining the rafts of ducks are other water birds—the American coot; the eared grebe and its larger cousin, the western grebe; the great blue heron and a number of its smaller kin; the American avocet; black-necked stilt; white pelican; a gallery of smaller wading and shorebirds; a number of terns and gulls, including the black tern, one of the Audubon Society's blue-listed species.

▲

Lark bunting perched amidst thistles. The arsenal offers bird-watchers the closest location to Denver for viewing Colorado's state bird. Ground nesting songbirds such as the western meadowlark use high perches as calling posts. These posts overlook the bird's established territory, and their visibility serves to warn other males to stay away. ▶

Following this moveable feast are other raptors—golden eagles, ospreys, prairie falcons, goshawks, merlins, Swainson's hawks, roughlegs, harriers, Cooper's hawks, sharpshins, and the endangered peregrine falcon. Few of these birds stay year round at the arsenal, but taken together, they provide a spell-binding procession spring and fall, a changing of the guard that is easily missed in the cataleptic life of a big city.

Complications

Clean-up at the arsenal. Workers involved in interim clean-up projects wear protective clothing while in contaminated areas. ▶

◀ *Golden eagle at sunrise. This eagle is using a pole placed by arsenal employees specifically for raptor perch sites.*

Prairie dogs and dieldrin, eagles and DDE. The arsenal offers one of the strangest juxtapositions in the history of conservation—it is a wildlife refuge protected by poison. For wildlife, the advantages of this irony are obvious to anyone who has taken the time to contemplate the urban sprawl that laps at the western and southern borders of the arsenal. The disadvantages are less visible to the general public but no less profound.

Managers at the arsenal noticed the side effects of their manufacturing as early as the late 1940s. Reports of dead animals scattered along the margins of the arsenal lakes and disposal basins were commonplace. Workers also saw birds in the last extremities of

poisoning, swimming in tight, aimless circles, colliding with windows and walls, seized with convulsions. In 1959, a technician estimated that a minimum of 20,000 ducks had died on the Lower Lakes in the previous decade of "unknown causes." Analysis of dead waterfowl in the mid-fifties turned up one possible cause—high levels of pesticides in tissues. Wildlife losses through the Sixties and into the mid-Seventies continued in the same chilling vein: March 28, 1962—more than 100 ducks found dead of pesticide poisoning; spring, 1966—163 ducks dead; April, 1973—136 ducks dead; May 16, 1973—fish kill in the Lower Lakes; May 2, 1975—291 water birds dead. Songbirds, shorebirds, pheasants, birds of prey, even toads and frogs were found dead in and around the Lower Lakes and disposal basins.

And the problem reached far below the surface. In 1951, farmers north of the arsenal found that the groundwater they were using for irrigation actually damaged their crops. By 1957, nearby residents began to be concerned about the quality of their drinking water; soon after, Adams County citizens filed five claims against the Army for polluting their wells.

Since the first discovery of groundwater contamination, public concern has justifiably been focused on that major health issue. A critical issue in the Eighties has been the presence of trichloroethylene (TCE) in groundwater north of the arsenal. TCE is strongly

Magpie nests in barbed wire fence. A protective barrier encircling a toxic storage yard becomes a suitable nest site for black-billed magpies.

Prairie dog family. Having a complex and highly structured social order, prairie dogs learn when young to defer to stronger and more aggressive members of the colony.

suspected as a cancer-causing agent in humans. Work on this contamination has discovered four "plumes" of TCE pollution drifting north in groundwater toward the South Platte River. Some of the TCE comes from sources at the arsenal; the rest seems to emanate from sources to the south of the post. A groundwater treatment system has recently been installed in an effort to contain the arsenal's share of the pollution.

TCE-laced water is an obvious human health concern. Wildlife on the arsenal faces a much different, much nearer threat, however. Among the many toxic chemicals causing historic wildlife losses on the area have been dieldrin and aldrin, two potent insecticides manufactured for years on the arsenal. Like DDT, these compounds are very stable in the environment and in animal tissues. They remain highly poisonous for decades and tend to accumulate in animal fat. As a result, both can "biomagnify." By eating tiny amounts over a long period of time, an animal can build up dangerous amounts of either poison, and these residues can be further concentrated as they pass up the food chain to predators like hawks or eagles.

This has happened in some birds of prey on the arsenal. Golden eagles, red-tailed and

ferruginous hawks, and great-horned owls have been found dead on the area, victims of lethal doses of various pollutants. Research on kestrels at the arsenal found detectable levels of dieldrin in about half the eggs and young analyzed; DDE was detected in 1 of 33 samples. One coyote and a badger have been found dead on the arsenal, apparent victims of the accumulation of dieldrin. Prairie dogs around Basin A have been removed because they carried pesticide burdens that were potentially dangerous to predators. Death of avian and mammalian predators combined with analysis of a variety of prey species on the arsenal shows beyond doubt that aldrin-dieldrin contamination is a serious problem on some parts of the area. However, deer at the arsenal seem to have escaped serious exposure to toxics. Of fourteen deer sampled at the arsenal, only one suffered any detectable level of contamination.

There is a trend in this record of wildlife contamination that leaves room for cautious optimism. As major waste basins have been drained and waste products have been set aside, wildlife deaths have fallen off dramatically. With continued clean-up, we may see a time when wildlife at the arsenal will find refuge from poisons as well as from the crush of urban sprawl.

WHEN
Nature
HEALS

45

Questions Looking for Answers

Grasshopper. Grasshoppers and other insects constitute a food source for many creatures, among them reptiles, hawks, kestrels, burrowing owls, pheasants, grassland songbirds, coyotes and small rodents. ▶

▲

Running whitetail does. White-tailed deer are capable of tremend-ous running leaps. They are grace- *ful and elegant whether dashing off or standing alert.*

The arsenal's future is still being charted. There is universal agreement that it should be "cleaned up," but the consensus ends there. The question, "How clean is clean?" is still to be answered. Certainly clean enough to end groundwater contamination and the human health risks entailed in that contamination. Probably clean enough that an eagle or ferruginous hawk can spend a lifetime there without facing a premature death as a result of pesticide poisoning. But should we set a standard of decontamination that would be safe for hotels, restaurants, suburban homes? Should we make the arsenal clean enough so that "kids can eat the dirt," as one official has suggested? Colonel Daniel Voss, commander of Army operations at the arsenal, has observed that surrounding landholders and communities "should have to live up to the same standards we are held to here." He has a point. Are we willing to accept standards for airports, industries, wheat fields, and housing developments as stringent as those we impose on the arsenal?

There are two other points worth considering in the "how clean is clean?" controversy. The first is whether people will re-occupy the arsenal on the strength of guarantees from engineers, biologists, and public health officials that there is no risk. The second is whether we can afford a no-holds-barred, down-to-the-last molecule clean-up. Various sources have estimated the cost of a complete arsenal clean-up at

▲

Running white-tailed deer. The waving white flag of its tail is a delightful sight, readily identify-ing it from the more common and less wary mule deer.

$2-6 billion. Experience so far has shown that clean-up costs have been consistently under-estimated. Some observers have speculated that the cost could approach $15-20 billion before the job is done. The Department of Defense alone has forty-two Superfund sites, and there are more than 400 other sites that may need Superfund attention. What we would like to accomplish at the arsenal may have little to do with the final decision on clean-up—we may have created an environmental problem bigger than our bank account.

The management of wildlife on the arsenal is bound to be controversial. Endangered species like the bald eagle carry with them special constraints which complicate any wildlife program. In this case, the situation is particularly tangled since the arsenal prairie dogs, primary winter food source of the eagles, are subject to periodic outbreaks of sylvatic plague which, as we found in 1988-1989, can and do decimate their numbers. Insulating the eagles against an unexpected failure of local prey could prove difficult.

The area's deer are also likely to present difficulties. The population on the arsenal has been self-regulating in a sense, since the deer are free to come and go as their own perception of the situation dictates.

▲

Mule deer on skyline. The juxtaposition of skyscraper and mule deer is another of the surprises found at the arsenal. Despite contaminants and clean-up, the locality's twenty-seven square miles support over 300 mule and white-tailed deer.

Should managers try to maintain corridors for these movements, or should they take more direct control of the situation by fencing in the herd? A contained deer population could threaten the vegetation of the entire arsenal unless controlled. Adequate deer control measures can be hard to find. Relocating the deer would be an expensive and temporary solution, even assuming that someone in the West wants a truckload of new deer every fall. The most cost-effective approach would be to shoot the excess animals, but such techniques could be hard to defend with the whole Denver metropolitan area watching just over the fence. On the other hand, an uncontained deer herd without adequate movement corridors could cause significant traffic and damage problems in nearby urban areas.

Seemingly simple issues like the management of prairie dogs and jackrabbits even take on serious overtones if area managers are trying to re-establish native plants. A thriving jackrabbit population can digest new vegetation as fast as it's planted. And there are other possibilities that could further cloud decisions—reintroduction of bison, antelope, and elk; establishment of an experimental population of black-footed ferrets; construction of a large marsh on the upper end of First Creek.

▲

Prairie dog alarm call. Prairie dogs have a complex and varied communication system.

▲

Whitetail fawn. Fawns are a certain sign of summer's arrival. Typically born in June, their spots and copper-colored coats are gradually shed to make way for heavy brown winter coats.

A 17,000-acre reserve seems like a huge place, but, by the standards of a prairie ecosystem which developed in an ocean of space, it is tiny. Successful wildlife management on the arsenal will require a good overall grasp of the area's limitations as well as its current and potential relationships with nearby natural features like Barr Lake and the South Platte. Wildlife management decisions in a rapidly growing urban area like northeast Denver can often be made only once. There is little room for mistakes.

Of course, concerns over managing wildlife on the arsenal are based on a huge assumption—that the arsenal will continue to exist. Once the area is clean enough for wildlife, it will probably also be clean enough for warehouses, truck terminals, and any number of other specialized industrial installations. Right now, the Army seems inclined to hold onto the arsenal forever to avoid potential liability problems. But, if they were ever forced to sell, the economic advantages of classic "development" on the area are clear enough.

The dollar arguments on the side of wildlife are more vague, although they may be as telling. A hundred bald eagles, a hundred ferruginous hawks, a herd of trophy mule deer

▲

Coots on lake. Coots are more

likely to dart for sanctuary in the

marshy edges of a lake than to

take to the air to evade danger.

These diving birds are the most

abundant arsenal waterfowl.

within a stone's throw of Denver's airport and an easy bus ride from downtown could certainly translate into black ink in somebody's ledger.

A recent study of eagle watchers in Iowa showed that people were willing to drive more than 100 miles from home to get a bald eagle in their spotting scopes. On one official "bald eagle weekend," 3,500 visitors descended on an Iowa hamlet and spent $76,000 on gas, food, and lodging, all in the interest of seeing a white-headed bird. Spending patterns like these could become important to the communities around the arsenal. And, at the rate natural areas are disappearing, the wild experience offered there will only appreciate in value as we enter the next century.

So much for economics. We've developed a distasteful habit of making all our decisions with a ledger in one hand and a calculator in the other. For most of our history, we've been guided solely by the profit or loss in a transaction. In the last generation, we've replaced that hard-headed Yankee style of decision-making with a more bureaucratic approach, the benefit-cost ratio. Whatever the mathematical permutations, we continue to believe that numbers will make decisions we refuse to make for ourselves.

▲

Osprey with bluegill in talons.

Feeding on live fish, osprey hunt

the lakes of the arsenal as they mi- *grate through in spring and fall.*

The nineteenth-century playwright Oscar Wilde once observed that a cynic is "a man who knows the price of everything and the value of nothing." It's an apt description of the American attitude toward wilderness in the last 400 years. We've always been shrewd brokers, able to read the profit in a piece of untamed ground down to the decimal. What we've failed to grasp is the ultimate worth of wildness itself. Decisions like the ones we face at Rocky Mountain Arsenal are, in many ways, a test of how much we've grown in our time on this continent. We've established to the last red cent the price of an acre of asphalt. It remains to be seen whether we know the value of an eagle.

▲

Immature bald eagle. This bird was captured by the U.S. Fish & Wildlife Service as part of the Bald Eagle Management Project. It was measured, weighed, and fitted with a radio transmitter prior to release.

Black-tailed jackrabbit against a snowy background. The rabbit has found a sunny, warm spot early on a winter day. ▶

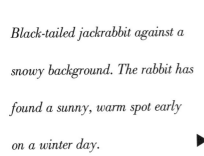

▲

Ducks at sunrise. Lakes at the arsenal provide habitat for a variety of water birds and aquatic organisms, including largemouth bass and northern pike. Adjacent stands of cattails are home for wetland species, such as muskrats, night-herons, and rails.

CODA:
OTHERS LOOK AT ROCKY MOUNTAIN ARSENAL

Western Wallflower

(*Erysimum asperum*) ▶

"Rocky Mountain Arsenal represents a once in a lifetime opportunity to develop one of our nation's most significant urban wildlife refuges."

—*National Wildlife Federation*

"To see nature's splendor amid this industrial folly makes me appreciate the wonderful resilience of our planet."

—*Representative*
Patricia Schroeder

"Keeping the entire 27 square miles as natural open space for eagles and hawks, badgers, prairie dogs, and deer will preserve Denver's western heritage and make it unique among American cities."

—*Denver Audubon Society*

Prairie Coneflower

(*Ratibida columnifera*) ▶

"Rocky Mountain Arsenal offers one of the nation's most outstanding wildlife viewing opportunities, in part because of its close proximity to a major metropolitan area."

—Perry Olson, Director,

Colorado Division of Wildlife

"The size of Rocky Mountain Arsenal provides a unique opportunity to maintain a diverse habitat which will promote dispersal of many wildlife species to smaller habitat patches throughout a metropolitan region."

—James G. Teer, President,

the Wildlife Society

"From a personal perspective, the wildlife at Rocky Mountain Arsenal adds a lot to my job. Few people have an opportunity to see bald eagles, deer, coyotes, and other such pleasant surprises on their way to work each morning. I'm a native Coloradan. I grew up out of doors on a farm, fascinated by animals. Wildlife is a large part of what makes Colorado so special and it deserves our continuing protection."

—Colonel Daniel Voss,

United States Army

WHEN
Nature
HEALS

55

BIBLIOGRAPHY

Meadow Salsify

(*Tragopogon dubius*) ▶

◀ Yawning burrowing owl. Perched

on a high point near its burrow,

this small owl dozed off one quiet

morning. This species stands about

10 inches high and is the only

North American owl capable of

digging a hole for nesting, though

it typically moves into prairie dog

holes instead.

EBASCO Services, Inc. 1989. "Black-tailed prairie dog activity survey for Rocky Mountain Arsenal." (Interim Report, June).

Environmental Science and Engineering, Inc. 1988. "Bald eagle study: Winters 1986–1987, 1987–1988." (Final Report, Version 3.1, September).

Environmental Science and Engineering, Inc. 1989. "Biota Remedial Investigation Final Report for Rocky Mountain Arsenal." (Version 3.2, May).

MK-Environmental Services, Inc. 1989. "Aquatic resources of Rocky Mountain Arsenal, Adams County, Colorado." (Final Report, August).

MK-Environmental Services, Inc. 1989. "Wildlife resources of Rocky Mountain Arsenal, Adams County, Colorado." (Final Report, September).

MK-Environmental Services, Inc. 1989. "Vegetation resources of Rocky Mountain Arsenal, Adams County, Colorado." (Final Report, October).

U.S. Fish and Wildlife Service. 1989. "The potential effects of Rocky Mountain Arsenal cleanup activities and Denver metropolitan transportation on bald eagles." (First Annual Progress Report, June).

Walsh, James P. & Associates, Inc. 1988. "Soil investigation and inventory of the Rocky Mountain Arsenal, Adams County, Colorado." (Preliminary Report, October).

PLANT AND ANIMAL SPECIES OBSERVED AT ROCKY MOUNTAIN ARSENAL

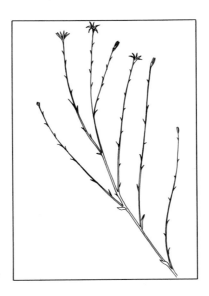

Skeleton Plant

(*Lygodesmia juncea*)

▶

TABLE A-1 MAMMALS OBSERVED OR POTENTIALLY PRESENT ON THE RMA

SORICIDAE
Masked shrew
Least shrew

VESPERTILIONIDAE
Small-footed myotis
Silver-haired bat
Big brown bat
Hoary bat

LEPORIDAE
Eastern cottontail
Desert cottontail
Black-tailed jackrabbit
White-tailed jackrabbit

SCIURIDAE
Thirteen-lined ground squirel
Spotted ground squirrel
Black-tailed prairie dog

Fox squirrel

GEOMYIDAE
Northern pocket gopher
Plains pocket gopher

HETEROMYIDAE
Silky pocket mouse
Olive-backed pocket mouse
Hispid pocket mouse
Plains pocket mouse
Ord's kangaroo rat

CRICETIDAE
Plains harvest mouse
Western harvest mouse
Deer mouse
Northern grasshopper mouse
Meadow vole
Prairie vole
Muskrat

ZAPODIDAE
Meadow jumping mouse

ERETHIZONTIDAE
Porcupine

CASTORIDAE
Beaver

MURIDAE
Norway rat
House mouse

CANIDAE
Coyote
Red fox
Swift fox
Gray fox

◀ *Rabbit runway. A snowy path between the arsenal and Denver's airport indicates the large number of cottontails and jackrabbits inhabiting the area.*

PROCYONIDAE
Raccoon

MUSTELIDAE
Short-tailed weasel
Long-tailed weasel
Mink
Badger
Striped skunk

CERVIDAE
Mule deer
White-tailed deer

ANTILOCAPRIDAE
Pronghorn

Source: MK-Environmental Services, Inc.

**TABLE A-2
BIRDS IDENTIFIED
ON THE RMA**

PODICIPEDIDAE
Pied-billed grebe
Eared grebe
Western grebe

PELECANIDAE
American white pelican

PHALACROCORACIDAE
Double-crested cormorant

ARDEIDAE
American bittern
Great blue heron
Snowy egret
Little blue heron
Black-crowned night-heron

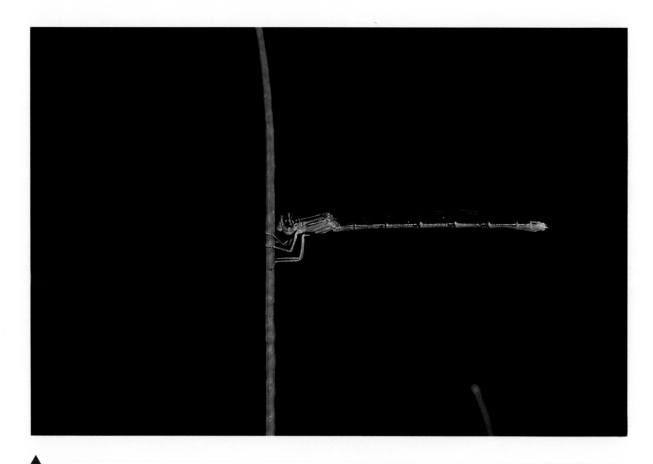

▲

Damselfly clinging to plant stem.

Feeding on insect larvae and

small crustaceans, damselflies in

turn are food for birds and fish.

THRESKIORNITHIDAE
White-faced ibis

ANATIDAE
Canada goose
Green-winged teal
Mallard
Northern pintail
Blue-winged teal
Cinnamon teal
Northern shoveler
Gadwall
American wigeon
Canvasback

Redhead
Ring-necked duck
Lesser scaup
Common goldeneye
Bufflehead
Hooded merganser
Common merganser
Ruddy duck

CATHARTIDAE
Turkey vulture

ACCIPITRIDAE
Osprey

Bald eagle
Northern harrier
Sharp-shinned hawk
Cooper's hawk
Swainson's hawk
Red-tailed hawk
Ferruginous hawk
Rough-legged hawk
Golden eagle
American kestrel
Prairie falcon

CRACIDAE
Ring-necked pheasant

▲

Fawn against shadows. A mule

deer fawn boldly ventures a short

distance from its mother.

◀ *Long-eared owl. One of the more difficult species to locate at the arsenal, long-eared owls are surprisingly numerous. They gather communally in Spring and nest in dense stands of trees.*

Full moon rising through eagle roost. Up to thirty bald eagles have been viewed using a communal night roost at the arsenal. A safe and undisturbed roost is an essential part of wintering bald eagle habitat. It is the loss of winter habitat which is of greatest risk to bald eagles. ▶

RALLIDAE
Virginia rail
Sora
American coot

CHARADRIIDAE
Killdeer

RECURVIROSTRIDAE
American avocet

SCOLOPACIDAE
Greater yellowlegs
Lesser yellowlegs
Solitary sandpiper
Willet
Spotted sandpiper
Western sandpiper
Least sandpiper
Pectoral sandpiper
Stilt sandpiper
Long-billed dowitcher
Common snipe
Wilson's phalarope

LARIDAE
Franklin's gull
Ring-billed gull
Herring gull

COLUMBIDAE
Rock dove
Mourning dove

CUCULIDAE
Yellow-billed cuckoo

STRIGIDAE
Eastern screech-owl
Great horned owl
Burrowing owl
Long-eared owl
Short-eared owl

CAPRIMULGIDAE
Common nighthawk

APODIDAE
Chimney swift

ALCEDINIDAE
Belted kingfisher

PICIDAE
Red-headed woodpecker
Yellow-bellied sapsucker
Downy woodpecker
Hairy woodpecker
Northern flicker

TYRANNIDAE
Western wood-pewee
Willow flycatcher
Dusky flycatcher
Cordilleran flycatcher
Say's phoebe
Western kingbird
Eastern kingbird

ALAUDIDAE
Horned lark

HIRUNDINIDAE
Tree swallow
Violet-green swallow

Northern rough-winged swallow
Cliff swallow
Barn swallow

CORVIDAE
Blue jay
Black-billed magpie
American crow

PARIDAE
Black-capped chickadee

SITTIDAE
Red-breasted nuthatch

White-breasted nuthatch

CERTHIIDAE
Brown creeper

TROGLODYTIDAE
House wren
Marsh wren

MUSCICAPIDAE
(SYLVIINAE)
Golden-crowned kinglet
Ruby-crowned kinglet

(TURDINAE)
Mountain bluebird
Townsend's solitaire
Swainson's thrush
Hermit thrush
American robin

MIMIDAE
Gray catbird
Northern mockingbird
Brown thrasher

MOTACILLIDAE
American pipit

▲

Ferruginous hawk. To shield its food from potential scavengers, a hawk mantles its wings around the meal. Magpies and crows generally come away with little more than scraps at most, but other hawks and eagles may displace the feeding raptor.

BOMBYCILLIDAE
Cedar waxwing

LANIIDAE
Northern shrike
Loggerhead shrike

STURNIDAE
European starling

VIREONIDAE
Solitary vireo
Warbling vireo
Red-eyed vireo

EMBERIZIDAE
(PARULINAE)
Tennessee warbler
Orange-crowned warbler
Nashville warbler
Northern parula
Yellow warbler
Chestnut-sided warbler
Yellow-rumped warbler
Blackburnian warbler

Blackpoll warbler
Black-and-white warbler
American redstart

Ovenbird
Northern waterthrush
MacGillivray's warbler
Common yellowthroat
Hooded warbler
Wilson's warbler
Yellow-breasted chat

(EMBERIZINAE)
Rose-breasted grosbeak
Black-headed grosbeak
Blue grosbeak
Lazuli bunting
Indigo bunting

Red-tailed hawk. An immature red-tailed hawk has come to feed on a cottontail which a golden ea- *gle killed but later abandoned after eating its fill.*

Dickcissel
Rufous-sided towhee
Cassin's sparrow
American tree sparrow
Chipping sparrow
Clay-colored sparrow
Brewer's sparrow
Vesper sparrow
Lark sparrow
Lark bunting
Savannah sparrow
Grasshopper sparrow
Fox sparrow
Song sparrow

Lincoln's sparrow
White-throated sparrow
White-crowned sparrow
Harris sparrow
Dark-eyed junco
McCown's longspur
Chestnut-collared longspur

(ICTERINAE)
Bobolink
Red-winged blackbird
Western meadowlark
Yellow-headed blackbird
Brewer's blackbird

Common grackle
Brown-headed cowbird
Northern oriole

FRINGILLIDAE
House finch
Pine siskin
Lesser goldfinch
American goldfinch

PASSERIDAE
House sparrow

(*Source: MK-Environmental Services, Inc.*)

Perched kingfisher. Belted kingfishers often hunt from favorite perches that afford a clear view of *wet areas containing small fish.*

TABLE A-3
REPTILES AND AMPHIBIANS OBSERVED OR POTENTIALLY PRESENT ON THE RMA

SNAKES

COLUBRIDAE
Plains garter snake
Common garter snake
Western terrestrial garter snake
Lined snake
Northern water snake
Western hognose snake
Milk snake
Bullsnake
Smooth green snake
Racer
Coachwhip

VIPERIDAE
Western rattlesnake

LIZARDS

SCINCIDAE
Many-lined skink

TEIIDAE
Six-lined racerunner

IGUANIDAE
Eastern fence lizard
Short-horned lizard
Lesser earless lizard

FROGS

HYLIDAE
Northern chorus frog

▲

Great horned owl babies. Colorado's earliest nesting bird is the great horned owl. Before trees leaf out in spring, it is possible to see the owlets as they grow large enough to branch, or wander, short distances away from the nest.

RANIDAE
Bullfrog
Northern leopard frog

TOADS

PELOBATIDAE
Plains spadefoot

BUFONIDAE
Woodhouse's toad
Great Plains toad

SALAMANDERS

AMBYSTOMATIDAE
Tiger Salamander

TURTLES

TRIONYCHIDAE
Spiny softshell

CHELYDRIDAE
Common snapping turtle

EMYDIDAE
Western box turtle

Painted turtle

Source: MK-Environmental Services, Inc.

**APPENDIX A
LIST OF TERRESTRIAL
PLANT SPECIES
OBSERVED AT ARSENAL**

ACERACEAE
Box-elder
Silver Maple

Great blue heron stretching. Herons stalk wetland shallows for fish, frogs, and invertebrates. Elusive and wary, they need considerable space to be secure. The lakes at the arsenal provide ample fishing opportunities for these wading birds.

AGAVACEAE
Spanish Bayonet

AMARANTHACEAE
White Pigweed
Sand Pigweed
Prostrate Pigweed
Rough Pigweed
Froelichia

ANACARDIACEAE
Skunkbrush Sumac

APOCYNACEAE
Dogbane

ASCLEPIADACEAE
Swamp Milkweed
Little Milkweed
Showy Milkweed
Whorled Milkweed
Green Milkweed

ASPARAGACEAE
Wild Asparagus

BIGNONIACEAE
Showy Catalpa

BORAGINACEAE
Fendler Cryptantha
Small Cryptantha
Sand Stickseed
Narrowleaf Gromwell

CACTACEAE
Ball Cactus
Hen-and-Chickens
Prickly Pear Cactus

▲

Fishing great blue heron. An expert fishing bird, this great blue is seeking fish and crayfish in a pond which is receding in the midsummer heat.

Wavy-leaf Thistle	False Boneset	Broom Butterweed
Bull Thistle	Prickly Lettuce	Three-tooth Groundsel
Horseweed	Blue Lettuce	Canada Goldenrod
Fetid Marigold	Blazing-star	Giant Goldenrod
Spreading Fleabane	Skeleton-weed	Missouri Goldenrod
Low Daisy	Silvery Tansy-aster	Soft Goldenrod
Western Goldenrod	Patterson Tansy-aster	Showy Goldenrod
Fluffweed	Ironplant Goldenweed	Perennial Sow-thistle
Cudweed	False Dandelion	Spiny Sow-thistle
Curlycup Gumweed	Scotch Thistle	Wire-lettuce
Broom Snakeweed	Plains Bahia	Common Dandelion
Annual Sunflower	Podospermum	Green-thread
Hairy Golden-aster	Prairie Coneflower	Yellow Salsify
Hymenopappus	Sombrero Coneflower	Cow-pen Daisy
Tall Marsh-elder	Platte Groundsel	Cocklebur

▲

Cottontail rabbit in snow. Shrubs provide enough natural shelter from the elements to permit rabbits to survive heavy snows and winds. They may also dig shallow burrows in the snow for increased pro- tection during severe weather.

CONVOLVULACEAE
Field Bindweed
Evolvulus
Bush Morning-glory

CRUCIFERAE
(BRASSICACEAE)
Desert Alyssum
Alyssum
Shepherd's-purse
White Top
Common Blue Mustard
Tansy-mustard
Western Tansy-mustard
Flixweed

White Draba
Western Wallflower
Prairie Peppergrass
Bladderpod
Cress
Tall Tumble-mustard
Tumble-mustard
Field Pennycress

CUCURBITACEAE
Wild Gourd

CUPRESSACEAE
Rocky Mountain Juniper
Tammy Juniper

CYPERACEAE
Threadleaf Sedge
Sun Sedge
Nebraska Sedge
Sedge
Galingale
Slender Spikerush
Common Spikerush
Great Bulrush
Chairmaker's Rush
Tule

▲

Canada geese. A small flock of geese walk across a partially frozen lake to an open section of water. There is safety and food available on and near arsenal lakes in winter.

ELAEAGNACEAE
Russian-olive

EQUISETACEAE
Scouring Rush

EUPHORBIACEAE
Snow-on-the-mountain
Spurge
Thyme-leaved Spurge
Croton

FUMARIACEAE
Golden Smoke

GERANIACEAE
Filaree, Crane's-bill

GRAMINEAE (POACEAE)
Crested Wheatgrass
Thickspike Wheatgrass
Fairway Crested Wheatgrass
Tall Wheatgrass
Quackgrass
Western Wheatgrass
Streambank Wheatgrass
Slender Wheatgrass
Redtop
Sand Bluestem
Fendler Three-awn

Red Three-awn
Sloughgrass
Side-oats Grama
Blue Grama
Smooth Brome
Japanese Brome
Cheatgrass
Buffalo Grass
Prairie Sandreed
Sand Bur
Windmill Grass
Feather Fingergrass
Bermuda Grass
Inland Saltgrass
Barnyard Grass

▲

Canada geese. Although it appears these geese have discovered a human swimming hole, they're actually on the way to their own pond, adjacent to the visitor center.

Canada Wildrye
Stinkgrass
Spreading Love-grass
Meadow Fescue
Foxtail Barley
Little Barley
Rice Cutgrass
Italian Rye-grass
Alkali Muhly
Marsh Muhly
Ring Muhly
False Buffalo Grass
Indian Ricegrass
Witchgrass
Switchgrass
Dallis Grass

Reed Canarygrass
Timothy
Kentucky Blue Grass
Sandberg Bluegrass
Rabbitfoot Grass
Tumblegrass
Cereal Rye
Green Foxtail
Squirreltail
Yellow Indiangrass
Prairie Cordgrass
Prairie Wedge-grass
Alkali Sacaton
Sand Dropseed
Needle-and-Thread
Green Needlegrass

Sixweeks Fescue

GROSSULARIACEAE
Golden Currant

HYPERICACEAE
Klamath Weed, St. Johnswort

JUNCACEAE
Baltic Rush

LABIATAE (LAMIACEAE)
False Pennyroyal
Water Horehound
Field Mint
Spearmint

▲

Whitetail doe feeding. Deer need a wide variety of foods to make their complex digestive system work properly. What appears to be random feeding is a behavior that ensures a balanced diet. New growth at the edge of a pond provides a special treat.

Horsemint
Catnip
Salvia
Germander

LEGUMINOSAE (FABACEAE)
Two-grooved Milkvetch
Pot-sherd Milkvetch
Ground Plum
Purple Milkvetch
Missouri Milkvetch
Honey Locust
Wild Licorice
Silvery Lupine
Alfalfa
White Sweetclover

Yellow Sweetclover
Colorado Locoweed
Compact Prairie-clover
Narrowleaf Scurfpea
Slimflower Scurfpea
New Mexico Locust
Black Locust
Sophora
Woolly Vetch

LEMNACEAE
Duckweed

LILIACEAE
Sand Lily
False Solomon's Seal

Death Camas

LOASACEAE
Evening-Star

MALVACEAE
Buttonweed
Scarlet Globemallow

MORACEAE
Mulberry

NYCTAGINACEAE
Sand Verbena
Narrowleaf Umbrella-wort
Heartleaf Umbrella-wort

▲

White pelicans frequent many   *arsenal's Lake Ladora.*

lakes in eastern Colorado during

spring and summer, including the

OLEACEAE
Green Ash
Common Lilac
Privet

ONAGRACEAE
Serrate Evening-primrose
Northern Willow-herb
Willow-herb
Scarlet Butterfly-weed
Small-flowered Butterfly-weed
Ground Smoke
Prairie Evening-primrose
Cutleaf Evening-primrose
Nuttall's Evening-primrose
Evening-primrose

PAPAVERACEAE
Prickly Poppy

PINACEAE
Blue Spruce
Austrian Pine
Ponderosa Pine
Scotch Pine

PLANTAGINACEAE
Narrowleaf Plantain
Pursh's Plantain

POLEMONIACEAE
Gilia

POLYGONACEAE
Annual Wild-buckwheat
Bushy Wild-buckwheat
Black Bindweed
Lady's Thumb
Smartweed
Knotweed
Branched Knotweed
Curly-leaf Dock
Willow-leaf Dock
Veiny Dock

PORTULACACEAE
Purslane

PRIMULACEAE
Fringed Loose-strife

RANUNCULACEAE
Western Virgin's Bower
Larkspur
Mousetail

ROSACEAE
Cinquefoil
Wild Plum
Chokecherry
Prairie Rose

Woods' Rose

SALICACEAE
White Poplar
Plains Cottonwood
Quaking Aspen
Peachleaf Willow
Coyote Willow

SANTALACEAE
Bastard Toadflax

SCROPHULARIACEAE
Butter-and-eggs
White Beardtongue
Narrowleaf Penstemon

Black-tailed jackrabbit feeding.

After several days of spring rains,

the fresh green growth is irresisti-

ble to arsenal herbivores such as

this jackrabbit.

Great Mullein
Water Speedwell

SOLANACEAE
Matrimony Bush
Ground Cherry
Buffalo Bur
Nightshade

TAMARICACEA
Tamarisk

TYPHACEAE
Narrowleaf Cattail
Broadleaf Cattail

ULMACEAE
American Elm
Siberian Elm
Hackberry

UMBELLIFERAE (APIACEAE)
Biscuit-root
Poison Hemlock

URTICACEAE
Stinging Nettle

VERBENACEAE
Fog Fruit
Creeping Charlie

VIOLACEAE
Yellow Violet

VITACEAE
Western Woodbine
Wild Grape

ZYGOPHYLLACEAE
Puncture Vine

Source: MK-Environmental Services, Inc.

▲

Backlit rabbit. Cottontails choose resting spots that offer clear lines of sight, an escape route, and per- *haps a ray of sun to warm them on chilly mornings. Staying relatively motionless is a way to avoid* *drawing the attention of a predator.*

Burrowing owl babies at edge of hole. Burrowing owls most often nest in abandoned prairie dog holes. The young owls frequently perch on the mound while waiting to be fed by their parents. ▶

▲

Northern oriole. A newly fledged oriole waits for a parent to bring food as it clings to a branch near its outgrown nest.

▲

Turkey vulture. The arsenal is a

stopover for vultures during their

fall migration.

▲

Populations of ring-necked phea-

sants at the arsenal probably re-

sulted both from introductions and

natural movement from nearby

farmland.

ROCKY MOUNTAIN ARSENAL

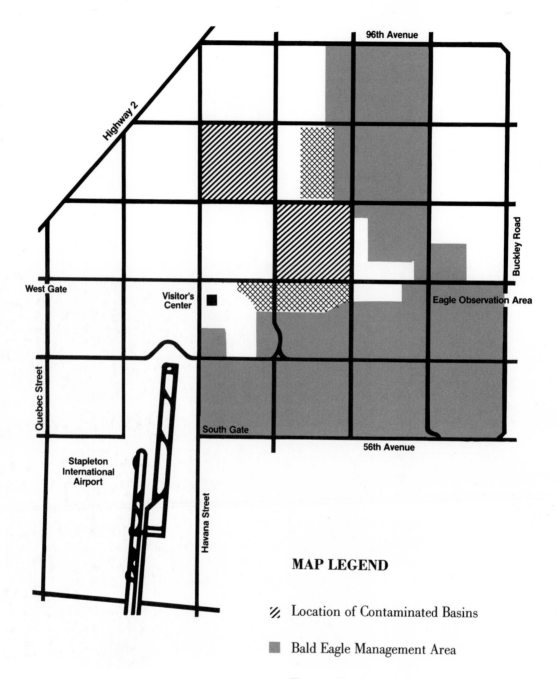

MAP LEGEND

Location of Contaminated Basins

Bald Eagle Management Area

Former Production Sites